Baby Led Weaning for Vegans:

60 Plant-Based Recipes for Babies and Kids That Adults Will Love

By
Cathleen Woods

ISBN-13:978-1974096893
ISBN-10:1974096890

Hi! I'm Cathleen, the mom, cook, writer, and photographer behind the Vegan Momma website and social media groups.

Baby led weaning was the perfect way for us to feed our daughters and it's what I recommend to all my friends who are starting out feeding their babies.

Why spoon feed purees when you can let your child explore and **feed themselves** on real, whole food? This method is not only easier on the parents, but it's what I think is best for our children long term.

One of the best things you can do for your children is give them **an amazing head start with healthy food**. When you start them out with a wide variety of fruits, vegetables, beans, whole grains, and nuts and seeds, their taste buds not only accept the new flavors, but also learn to **absolutely love those foods**.

I hope you love this guide to vegan baby led weaning as much as I loved writing it for you!

For more recipes, please visit Vegan Momma
www.vegan-momma.com

Contents

Baby Led Weaning Introduction

When I was a brand new parent, there was little about which I felt completely confident. There are dozens of subconscious decisions that you make daily that feel monumental at first. I remember holding my perfect newborn and feeling almost paralyzed with the fear that any one of those choices would lead us down a new path and wondering if it would create the best version of my baby possible.

The intensity of that new responsibility was overwhelming, but it relaxed over time as she got older and I knew I could never be anywhere close to perfect in my parenting. All I could really do was educate myself on the different options and go with my gut.

One of the very best decisions we made, and one that was instinctive and simple for me, was how she would eat. I knew I wanted her to be open-minded about food, able to eat in restaurants without major embarrassment, and to be in charge of how much she ate.

Those were my objectives before having kids, and as with many of those judgments we make when watching new parents as non-parents ourselves, it doesn't always end up working out the way we want. One of my favorite lines from Sex and the City was when Charlotte and Trey "tell each other the lie all expecting parents tell each other in order to procreate;" that their children would be different. I can't tell you how many things I thought I'd never do that I ended up doing, and often loving, when I was finally a parent.

But food was different. It was remarkably simple for me, and calm; without struggle.

One of the main reasons for this is because I learned about a method of feeding children called Baby Led Weaning. It's kind of a silly title as it has nothing to do with weaning.

My daughter didn't officially wean herself until she was more than three years old and I don't expect my second daughter will either. A more appropriate title would be "Baby Led Eating."

I didn't have a ton of experience watching mothers feed their children, and I was used to seeing the frenetic pureeing and spoon-feeding dance between parent and child. That progressed to the cutting into tiny pieces of food and then to the chicken nuggets and plain pasta phase, often accompanied by a parent cooking a second meal for their child.

Baby Led Weaning Introduction

I read about Baby Led Weaning and the parents feeding their babies what they were eating and it was a light bulb moment for me. YES! That's exactly what I'd wanted. I wanted my children to love food in the same way I do and I didn't want to create food challenges in my children that manifested in aversions or worse, disorders, as adults.

I would be in charge of what and where they ate, and they would be in charge of how much. I hope that later in life this means they will choose the "what" and "where" in a healthy way.

The basic premise of Baby Led Weaning is that you give your baby real food and over a period of many months they learn how to get it to their mouth, chew it (even without teeth), put it to the back of their mouth, and swallow it.

Yes, the "swallow it" is the part that gave me pause too. Wouldn't this put her at bigger risk of choking? There is nothing scarier in life than the prospect of your child in that type of danger, especially if it's a choice you're making that puts her in that position.

From what I read, **children who eat this way are possibly less likely to choke than a child fed purees** because when you eat a puree you suck and swallow rather than chew, so when they transition to those tiny chunks of food they suddenly have to manipulate their mouth in a different way. If they start with something that needs to be gummed they always know food needs to go down this way rather than slurped. I've heard from mothers who fed purees that there's always a scary period of gagging and sometimes choking.

With our first, I did not experience any choking, but we did have gagging. There's a big difference. Choking means there's little or no air getting past the piece of food. With gagging, it means the food has reached the gag reflex, which on babies is near the middle of their tongue, not as close to the throat as an adult's.

I have to admit that any time she gagged my head would spin in a way that I can only describe as almost blacking out. However, on the outside I remained calm and gave her encouraging looks and she always figured it out. That kind of learning is key to proper eating because she can see that when something is too big to go down it must come back in your mouth and be chewed more. Most of the time the piece of food was never close to being near her throat and in danger of choking.

Baby Led Weaning Introduction

Are we past this fear now? I made this jump with hesitation but acceptance. It was one of many things in my mom life that would cause me to picture awful scenarios, but one I accepted as part of learning and growing. It was also a very short period of time in her life, and after we got past it I felt incredibly confident that she could eat anything she wanted.

Many toddlers can't figure out how to eat a grape, and that puts them at a greater danger than a child who was fed real food from the beginning. She knew to chew whole nuts by the time she was a year old, whereas a puree-fed baby would just have been transitioning to tiny chunks of soft food at that point. She could eat tough cooked greens and entire pieces of spaghetti before she had teeth. And her method for each is hilarious. Spaghetti has a sucking and slurping that reminds me of Joey Chestnut on the Fourth of July, even with the same slight jumping motion to throw things down her throat.

So how do you do it? I remember reading a website on Baby Led Weaning and still coming away thinking, "Okay, so how do I do this?" Then I read a book on it and thought the same thing. What's the method? What's the plan? Teach me how so I can do it properly!

There just isn't much to it. It's that incredibly simple. Here's how…

You start with large pieces of real food that are soft. At first little to nothing actually gets in their mouth. Then a few days or weeks later some goes in their mouth but gets spit out. Then you'll notice that it seems some of the food is actually going down their throat, the clues being that either you can see them swallowing or there's a little gagging or there's a different texture or color in their diapers. Shortly after that they catch on that this food is fantastic! And that she wants more of it!

Along the way her motor skills are developing too, and I have to believe that eating this way helps to hone them more than just being fed with a spoon. There's an innate motivation to learn to eat and if she's in charge of the process she has more need to figure it out. Different hand and fingers skills develop over time during the course of the first months of eating.

Baby Led Weaning Introduction

The perfect compliment to eating during this period of time is mother's milk. I always nursed before feeding her, for two reasons. First, I wanted her to know that this was time to eat. I'd usually nurse her at the table to cement this association. We also always did this at the normal mealtimes.

Second, I did not want her to be frustrated and have a negative association with eating food. It was just a fun time for her. If she was still hungry afterwards, we'd nurse again. This would work just as well with a bottle fed baby.

Once you reach the stage where your baby is swallowing food and can use their hands to pick up anything they really want, you can progress to feeding them what you eat for dinner. The only thing to keep in mind is that you need to control the amount of sodium you give them. A diet that consists of mostly homemade vegan food is very unlikely to be high in sodium, so you probably have nothing to worry about.

The only modification I made to our diet at this point was that I didn't salt any of our meals while cooking them until she was 1-year old. My husband and I just salted at the table.

There are varying beliefs on allergens in a baby's diet. If you have strong family allergies, you will probably want to be careful about giving allergens like nuts, wheat, and soy as initial baby foods. I'll talk more about the allergy sensitive schedule I'd follow later in the book.

Some studies seem to say that early introduction actually has the opposite effect and creates a less sensitive child in the future. The AAP also now recommends feeding high-allergy foods early in your child's life.

How Much to Feed

I remember talking to a mom who was feeding purees with her 6 month old and a big question she had was how to know how much to feed her baby. I just shrugged and said, "when she's done." I regret that because it seems so smug looking back on it. It just wasn't an issue for me and I didn't realize at the time how much of a problem that is for most parents, going forward.

Baby Led Weaning Introduction

When my daughter is done eating, she's done. It's always been that way and always will be. She decides how much she eats. How could I ever decide that for another person? If you're eating proper foods, and you have no negative food issues, you know when you don't need or want to eat more and you stop.

I firmly believe that most of the "will power" struggles that we have as adults come from inappropriate food battles as children.

I never want to get in a situation where I'm coaxing my child to eat more. Just think about what that's saying to her on a subconscious level. "You don't know what's best for you. This will make you feel better. Eat just a little bit more." Some days she eats a few spoonfuls of something and says she's done. I will sometimes ask her if she's certain she ate enough and will remind her that we won't be eating anything until the next mealtime and will she be full enough until then. If she says yes, she's done. That's that.

We don't snack like many children we see. I don't judge parents who do this, mind you. It just doesn't work for us. If I give her snacks she just won't eat a full meal later, and I believe that a solid lunch or dinner is better than what I can offer her for a snack.

For us, it's one mid-afternoon snack, and as she got older we added in a morning snack. The only exception I make for this is on airplanes or long car trips.

Very rarely she'll say she's hungry before a mealtime and I just gently remind her that we're about to eat and that she needs to make sure she eats enough at that meal so she won't be hungry later.

This sounds like a hard line, but as a very gentle parent I just believe that I'm doing what's best for her body by helping her to focus on eating in a healthy way rather than counting on treats to fill her up. It's appropriate and important to feel hunger. I read once that obese people often never feel hungry because they eat more than they need.

In practice, what this means for my toddler is that some days she eats what I'd consider a full meal at all three meals of the day. Other days she seems to eat almost nothing for one, and on occasion there are two mealtimes where she eats very little and then she eats a massive third meal. It all seems to balance out, and the less of a deal I make it, the better.

Baby Led Weaning Introduction

I never say one is good eating and the other is poor, in fact I make little comment on it one way or the other. "Did you get enough to eat?" and sometimes, "did you eat enough to keep you full until lunchtime?" are the two questions I ask if she seems to have eaten very little.

I might say, "You weren't very hungry, were you?" I try to remain non-judgmental the entire time. If she eats a lot, "you were so hungry, weren't you? Maybe that's because you didn't eat as much at lunchtime."

Of course I've made mistakes. I could see myself getting into a habit of saying, "you need to eat a little more of dinner before we can have fruit," and I cut it short. I just didn't want to make a sweet thing contingent upon eating more food. That seems like a shortcut to having her swallow something just to get a treat, and that doesn't ring true to my general hope that she'll eat as much as she wants.

I also try to be careful about how I eat in front of her because I know she's modeling. If I eat too quickly or constantly finish my plate, I know she's going to try to do that. So, I slow down. I leave some on the plate and eat just until I feel done rather than trying to clean up. I let her know when I'm full and say no thank you to more food. If I want more, I say, "I'm still hungry so I am going to have some more food."

As for being a vegan baby, the natural question would be whether I take special care to ensure that she has a well balanced diet. Of course I do! And at the same time, no, not at all.

I want to put this out there. I eat what I want and as much as I want. However, what I want is what most people would consider incredibly healthy food.

The options that my daughter has for food include tons of vegetables, beans, whole grains, fruits, nuts and seeds, and healthy oils. It's how we naturally eat, and she can eat as much as she wants of any of that. Do I worry about it beyond that? Nope.

I have friends who are pediatricians who have said to me, "it's good you still breastfeed because they really need the calcium in milk." That is simply untrue. I don't feel a need to give her a non-dairy milk to make up the difference in her not drinking cow's milk like other kids do. She gets plenty of calcium from foods she loves like broccoli, Brussels sprouts, kale, carrots, cauliflower, sweet potatoes, beans, tofu, figs, oranges, and raisins.

Baby Led Weaning Introduction

I can understand if you have a picky eater and you can't get them to eat vegetables. But I'm here to say this whole "get them to eat" and "don't like vegetables" thing can be avoided completely if they just eat these foods from the start. It's easier for our bodies to extract and use the calcium from plant-based foods than from cow's milk, so she probably gets more than an average healthy kid anyway.

My daughter has gone through phases where she says she does not like certain foods. I don't make a big deal out of this. In one particularly cute phase, she started telling us, "when I get older…" I will eat figs, or avocados, or green beans. We just agreed with her, and over time that often has happened.

There are two other things that I think really help with raising a child who appreciates food and never abuses it. One is that she helps me cook, almost for every meal. She helps cut things and we always talk about what we're doing and what's being added into the meals. Sometimes when we're eating she asks me to tell her what's in the meal.

The second thing is that we grow some of our food and we go see food being grown and pick it ourselves. This fundamental understanding of where food comes from is crucial to appreciating the entire process behind eating. If you know food grows from the ground, you not only treat the Earth better, but you recognize that something that comes from a box simply can't be of the same quality food. You will make an effort to incorporate as much real food into your life as possible.

I will warn you; baby led weaning is a gigantic, huge, incredible mess at first. Your baby will have food all over themselves, all over the table, the floor, and in places you would never think to imagine. I just needed to learn to relax and let it go. After it's all done you can clean. And by "all done," I mean in 18 years.

I did try to pick carefully at restaurants though. There was this one time with couscous that remains stuck in my brain for its utter embarrassment. I could not get the area cleaned up and we just kind of skittered out of there repeating our apologies. I recommend something a bit more solid for outings.

How to Begin Baby Led Weaning

6-Month Safety Guidelines

The current pediatric recommendation is that babies eat breastmilk only until 6 months old. I followed this and wholeheartedly believe in it. I also followed what I read about the physical requirements needed to start feeding baby, including that they need to be able to sit up completely on their own, have lost their tongue thrust, and that they need to be able to hold an object firmly in their hands. They need to sit up straight and slightly forward so that if they have to work something down their throat it goes in the correct direction. No leaning backwards.

Some people go by the "he's interested in food so I'll give it to him," but developmentally, they start to show interest in their surroundings around 4 months, so that doesn't necessarily mean they're ready to eat at that point. They should be able to pick up a toy and put it to their mouth in order for you to start feeding them.

Around this age your child will be able to grab things but can't yet open her hand on purpose to get to the rest of the food on the inside. This makes stick-shaped pieces of food perfect, as long as they stick out of the top of her hand so she can work on that section.

The eating at this point is all about playing, figuring things out, and eventually tasting. I've heard other moms getting frustrated at this point because they worry their child isn't actually eating anything, but that's exactly the point. They won't really start eating until around 9-12 months, although of course that can vary.

The idea is to start your children on a piece of real food that you're eating, like a pear, or a soft sweet potato, and let them figure out how to put it in their mouth. They are in charge, with you simply observing, monitoring, and encouraging.

Ideally you can feed them the same type of food you are eating, as long as it's cut in a proper shape for them to hold. I did always feed her at the same time as us. Mealtimes have always been together, and for our family this is very important. We take our time, don't get up until we're done, and we talk about our days together. The way to apply this right now is by giving an unsalted well-done version of what you are eating and allowing them to play without any rush from you.

How to Begin Baby Led Weaning

No one besides your baby should be putting food in her mouth. That is the fast road to choking. She has to be completely in charge of what and how much goes in her mouth, for many reasons but specifically so that she knows how to manipulate it safely.

The other main safety rule is that your baby must be observed at all times. Even a quick trip to the kitchen counter to grab something is enough time for your baby to choke. You can probably guess that this style of eating takes longer at first, but in my experience over the long run it significantly cuts down on the stress that many other families experience during mealtime.

I highly recommend that all parents take an infant CPR class so that you know what to do in the event of an emergency. You learn, for instance, that you never want to reach your hand into your child's mouth when they're gagging because it could cause the food to lodge in the windpipe or get stuck in the airway. They also teach you how to tell when your baby is gagging versus choking. With choking you want to intervene immediately, but with gagging you want to let your child work it out on her own. Again, a certified CPR professional is the best person to issue you these warnings, but you can also do some quick research online to get a general idea of the safety rules.

First Foods: 6 Months

What to Feed for the First Meal

The whole premise of Baby Led Weaning is that baby eats what the rest of the family is eating. This allows her to share in the community of eating together and expands her taste buds, but also allows her to look around and see how everyone else is handling each type of food. So, you can feed anything you're eating, as long as there isn't more than 400mg of sodium or honey in it. This section helps to give you an idea of how to cut the pieces of food you're offering to your newest eater.

Pears

I have fond memories of my daughter figuring out how to snare her pear on the side of the table so it couldn't roll around and she could bend her head down to eat it. She kept her hands on either side so it would slide left or right and the table prevented it from rolling forward, for the most part.

Peaches

If your baby is ready to start eating during peach season, this is a great treat for them. I'd peel the skin at the beginning because it can tend to be somewhat tough. You can let them figure out how to hold a small peach themselves, probably with a similar snaring trick to the one my daughter used.

Keep in mind that peaches and pears are two of the more popular methods of helping to move digestion along (if you know what I mean), so if you start noticing runnier poop and she's been eating a lot of peach, pear, or plum, you might want to cut back or space them out a little more.

Sweet Potatoes

I baked my sweet potatoes until they were nice and soft and cut them into long stick shaped pieces that she could hold onto and put to her mouth. She would also just pick up the whole potato and bite at it. She still loves eating sweet potatoes like this; like a comic strip drumstick.

Butternut Squash

Well-cooked squash is a great starter food for Baby Led Weaning. I tried to stay away from the very stringy parts of the squash and from things like acorn and spaghetti squash until she was more confident after a few months of eating.

Avocados

I sometimes kept avocados whole, but usually cut into finger-shaped strips for her to grab. You can peel it and let them gum the fruit and suck it in.

Apples

At first the best thing you can do with apples is to bake them until they're very soft and let them chew on them. In a few months you can offer a whole apple that they can gnaw on themselves. I personally stayed away from cut apples for several months because it's easy for a small chunk to break off and get lodged in their throat.

One trick I loved with pears and cooked apples was to cut the core out of the middle so she could learn to hook her fingers through the hole and hold the fruit steady.

Bananas

A popular way to give babies bananas is by keeping the peel on most of it and just cutting a chunk of peel off, so your baby has a section she can eat and a section to hold the banana steady. You can also split the banana into thirds down the middle and give a small finger-shaped piece for baby to hold onto and eat.

First Foods: 7-9 Months

Opening Hands on Purpose

Sometime around 7-9 months you'll notice that your baby can start opening her hand on purpose. She might start squeezing food in her fists and sucking out the squished part. Before this, she'd likely just drop the piece of food in her hand so she could get a new piece, but now she's able to open the current hand and shove things in her mouth. If your baby has teeth, this is a great time to start offering crunchier vegetables like celery and bell peppers. At this point you can start giving chunks of cooked vegetables, crunchier foods, hummus, and even a spoon for dipping.

Broccoli and Cauliflower

My daughter loved broccoli from the very beginning. I would cook them more than usual so they were nice and soft and I always kept a large piece of stem on them so she could hold it. Broccoli has a different texture than most of the other first foods I fed her and I think it makes for great learning. You'll really notice this in her diaper when she has started swallowing.

Celery

I gave large sticks of celery and just pulled off the strings. She loved to dip the sticks in hummus.

Hummus

I recommend making hummus because it's so simple and you can control every ingredient. I made my standard hummus recipe but just left out the salt. You can also make different bean spreads to allow your child to taste a variety of different beans.

Soup

Perfect soups at this stage are split pea, broccoli "cheddar," potato leek, butternut squash, and other puree multidimensional soups. This is when I started giving her exactly what we ate

First Foods: 7-9 Months

for dinner, and I simply did not salt the soup on the stove. My husband and I added it at the table. You can offer her pre-loaded spoons of the soup so she learns to feed herself.

Pineapple

Chunks of pineapple can break off rather easily, so closely monitor her eating this food. Everyone loves pineapple though. I liked to cut wedges that she could hold onto and chew. Some people keep the rind on the wedge so their baby has a nice handle.

Melons

This is a good time to start offering melons. I found that larger chunks were again the best option here. A piece about the width of a banana and perhaps 4 inches long was the perfect size for my daughter.

Green Beans

I have a great recipe for green beans with olive oil and garlic that is a huge hit in my house, but you can also just steam them at the beginning. Cook them slightly longer than you might normally, so they're not going to break off in her hand but so that she can gum or gently chew them.

Asparagus

Asparagus is basically the perfect size and with a perfect texture for learning how to navigate stringier foods at this age.

Edamame

Non-GMO, organic edamame beans that are unsalted are perfect foods for you baby to eat right now. You can pop them out of the shells or show how to do it themselves.

First Foods: 8-10 Months

Adding in Foods at 8-10 Months

Once she's about 8 to 10 months old, she'll start using her fingers to pick up her food. This is when you can start offering smaller things like blueberries, raspberries, beans, and smaller pasta. She will also probably be ready to try using a fork to stab food and can certainly use a spoon on runnier things like soups and dips. Preloaded forks are great at this age to start teaching how to use utensils.

Grapes

Any small fruit like grapes, cherry tomatoes, cherries, small strawberries need to be cut in quarters lengthwise. Foods shaped like little balls I waited on for a few months; probably closer to 10 months old.

Blueberries

I would smash the blueberry before giving it to her until I was totally sure she knew to chew every single time. This way if she swallowed without chewing she wouldn't choke on the berry.

Other Berries

Strawberries can cause allergic reactions, so keep it in mind when your baby eats them. Raspberries and blackberries are soft enough that they should basically melt in their mouth, and they're likely to be squished a little in their fingers before entering their mouth. Just observe to be sure she is manipulating them properly.

Lettuce

Lettuce is easier to eat than cooked greens and it has a fun crunch. The thing to keep in mind is that it can take up a lot of space in their belly and it won't really fill them up. So when your child is eating much more solid food, try to limit the amount of foods like this that aren't dense in calories. I recommend offering the crunchy sections until your child figures out eating the looser leaves.

First Foods: 8-10 Months

Kale and Other Greens

Kale is one of those foods that you might just assume your baby will not be able to eat. When you chew it, it takes on a different texture in your mouth and you then have to really chew it to make it small enough to swallow. I've seen toddlers and some adults who just can't eat greens. My daughter didn't have trouble with it though. I remember giving it to her and watching her like a hawk and she just ate it like everything else. She still loves it.

I think a key is to scrunch the kale to make it nice and pliable until they have more teeth to really be able to rip at it. I have a few raw kale salads recipes in this book that she loves. You can also cook greens and just let them bite big chunks, or chop them up and let them take as much as they want.

Beans

The safest bet is to make your own beans here, so you can control the salt content. You can also find canned beans made without salt, but it's typically more difficult. The key again is to offer a wide variety so she can get used to all the different flavors and textures of beans.

Raisins and Dried Fruit

This is a good time to give raisins a try; just monitor and make sure she isn't having trouble swallowing them. My daughter loved dried fruit like mangos, bananas, and other fruit leathers at this stage. They're fun to tear into and can make a nice snack going forward.

Whole Grain Pasta

Quinoa was our first whole grain. I used organic, non-GMO quinoa and other whole grains that I rinsed before cooking.

I offered her first pasta around 10 months old. This was a difficult decision for me. I knew I didn't want to give her white pasta, but I am also not ecstatic about wheat either. There are tons of stories about the high amounts of arsenic in rice, so I also was concerned about gluten-free pasta made from rice.

First Foods: 8-10 Months

In the end I started her with organic whole wheat pasta, in a variety of shapes. The funniest to me was the spaghetti, which she eats by sucking a strand down her throat. There seems to be little chewing involved and watching it can be terrifying, but she's never had even a small problem gagging on spaghetti.

I don't give her plain pasta, unless I'm having a terrible day and am desperate at dinnertime. She's always had some kind of sauce on it, which is my way of making sure it's healthy.

Tofu and Tempeh

Soybeans can be another allergen, so we waited until around 10 months as well and introduced it slowly. There's debate on the healthfulness of soy products, and we don't eat much of it, but we make sure what we eat is non-GMO and organic.

You can bake, pan-fry, sauté, or use any other method you normally use with tofu and feed it to your baby. They will likely love it, especially since it can take on so many different flavors.

First Foods: 9-12 Months

Pincher Grip

Somewhere between 9 and 12 months you'll notice that her pincher grip has really developed, and she can pick up tiny things like pieces of rice with her thumb and forefinger.

At this point she can typically eat basically anything you give her with observation and, of course, depending on the child. Somewhere in the next few months she'll also get pretty good at using silverware, which will be an impressive trick for the grandparents to watch (just don't make her perform!)

Be careful with added salt until at least a year, and then keep it in moderation just like for everyone in the family.

Now the fun begins and you can eat the exact same meals all the time without having to worry as much about cutting the right shapes!

*Quick note: In the recipes I use canned things like tomatoes and beans because they are easy and convenient. You can always substitute in fresh tomatoes, homemade vegetable stock, or your own rinsed and cooked beans. Just keep the measurements the same.

Pumpkin Oat Pancakes

These are gluten-free and packed with nutrients.
They're perfect on a cool winter morning.

Pumpkin Oat Pancakes

Ingredients

1 c. rolled oats

1 c. pumpkin puree (not pie filling)

¼ c. almond milk

2 Tbsp. coconut oil

1 Tbsp. lemon juice

1 tsp. maple syrup

6 Tbsp. aquafaba (liquid from a can of beans) or 2 flax eggs (2

Tbsp. flax mixed into 6 Tbsp. water until frothy)

1 tsp. vanilla

½ tsp. baking soda

½ tsp. salt (omit for under 1 years old)

1 tsp. cinnamon

½ tsp. ginger

¼ tsp. nutmeg

Instructions

1. Put the oats in a blender or food processor and pulse until it turns into flour. Add the rest of the ingredients and pulse until they're combined.

2. Warm a griddle or saucepan to medium-high heat and add in a small amount of coconut oil or olive oil to grease the pan. Put ¼ cup size dollops of batter down on the pan and cook until you start to see bubbles, about 3 minutes. Flip the pancakes and cook the other side for another 3 minutes, or until the pancakes are lightly golden brown.

3. This batter can get a bit thick towards the bottom so you can add more almond milk to thin the pancakes out.

Serves 4

Buckwheat Blueberry Pancakes

You can use any gluten-free whole grains you like for this recipe, and you can also sub in any fruit. We love strawberries, blackberries, diced peaches, and even pears in this recipe.

Buckwheat Blueberry Pancakes

Ingredients

1 c. buckwheat flour

1 c. barley flour (or oat, brown rice, whole wheat)

2 tsp. baking powder

½ tsp. sea salt

2 c. almond milk

¼ c. ground flaxseeds

3 Tbsp. coconut oil, melted

2 Tbsp. maple syrup

1½ tsp. vanilla extract

1½ c. frozen or fresh blueberries

Instructions

1. Preheat a skillet over medium heat.

2. In a large bowl, combine the flours, baking powder, and sea salt.

3. In a large measuring cup, combine the milk, flaxseeds, coconut oil, maple syrup, and vanilla and whisk to combine.

4. Add the wet ingredients into the dry and stir just until combined and so there are no large lumps left. Gently fold in the blueberries.

5. Lightly oil your skillet with coconut oil. Use a ¼ cup measure to divvy out the pancake batter on the skillet. Cook for about 3 minutes on one side, until bubbles appear and the edges start to dry out. Flip and cook for another 3 minutes on the remaining side.

Serves 4-6

Scramble with Roasted Potatoes & Shiitake Bacon

This may seem like a lot of steps, but this is a super easy meal. You can bake the potatoes and mushrooms together and they take less than a minute to prepare. This is also a really simple tofu scramble that require no chopping; it's just spices stirred in to the mixture. It makes a delicious weekend meal for your toddler and the whole family.

Ingredients for Tofu Scramble

1 package organic firm tofu

1 Tbsp. olive oil

2 Tbsp. nutritional yeast

½ tsp. garlic powder

½ tsp. onion powder

¼ tsp. sea salt

¼ tsp. turmeric

¼- ½ tsp. black salt (to taste) (leave out for younger than 1 years old)

3 Tbsp. low-sodium vegetable broth

Instructions for Scramble

1. Over medium heat in a skillet, add the olive oil and crumble the tofu into the pan. Add the nutritional yeast and spices and stir until it's combined.

2. Add in the vegetable broth and bring it to a quick boil and then lower the heat, stirring to mix the broth into the tofu. This gives it a nice creamy texture. Taste for seasoning and serve.

Scramble with Roasted Potatoes & Shiitake Bacon

Ingredients for Roasted Potatoes

1 small potato per person

1 tsp. olive oil per potato

pinch of salt and pepper

herbs you like (thyme or herbs de Provence are really nice here)

Instructions for Roasted Potatoes

1. Preheat the oven to 350° F.

2. Cut the potatoes into nice holding pieces, or use whole fingerling potatoes to make it even easier. Place the potatoes on a baking sheet and coat with olive oil, salt

Ingredients for Shiitake Bacon

1 pound of shiitake mushrooms (you can use regular white mushrooms, crimini, or portobella)

Olive oil to drizzle on

Salt and pepper

Instructions for Shiitake Bacon

1. Preheat the oven to 350° F.

2. Slice the shiitakes into thin pieces and place them on the baking sheet. Coat with olive oil, salt, and pepper and bake for 30 minutes or until crispy. You'll probably need to turn them once about halfway through baking. You can cook these on the same baking sheet as the potatoes.

Serves 4

Apple Pie Oatmeal

We love warm fall flavors on a cold day and this oatmeal is simple and hits the spot. Cooking softens the apples and allows them to absorb the flavor of the cinnamon.

Apple Pie Oatmeal

Ingredients

2 c. filtered water

1 c. organic rolled oats

1 apple, diced

2 Tbsp. ground flax seeds

1 tsp. ground cinnamon

¼ c. raisins, optional

Instructions

1. Bring the water to a boil and then add the oats and apple chunks. Bring the water back up to a boil, stir everything, and then reduce the heat to a simmer and cover.

2. Cook for about 10 minutes, until the water is nearly absorbed and the oats and apples are soft.

3. At this stage I like to turn the heat off and stir vigorously until the oats break down and get very creamy. Add in the remaining ingredients and serve warm.

Serves 2-4

Blueberry Banana Overnight Oats

You can flavor overnight oats with absolutely any fruit and spices you like. This recipe makes 1 serving, but you can multiply as many times as you like to serve more people.

Blueberry Banana Overnight Oats

Ingredients

½ c. organic rolled oats

½ c. nondairy organic milk

¼ tsp. ground cinnamon

¼ c. frozen or fresh blueberries

1 Tbsp. chia seeds

¼ banana, mashed

Instructions

1. In a small mason jar, combine all the ingredients and shake it all together. Store in the refrigerator overnight and eat in the morning.

2. I prefer the flavor of fresh bananas rather than ones that have been cut and have sat out, so I just add my fruit in the morning rather than letting them soak overnight. Test it out to see what you prefer.

Serves 1

Carrot Cake Muffins

These muffins are hearty but flavorful, and super fun to make with your children. I love the warm spices and fluffiness of them. I know they use a lot of ingredients, but they're simple to make.

Carrot Cake Muffins

Ingredients

2 c. oat flour

2 Tbsp. flax meal

6 Tbsp. warm water

2 tsp. baking powder

1½ tsp. cinnamon

1 tsp. baking soda

½ tsp. nutmeg

½ tsp. ginger

¼ tsp. salt

½ c. applesauce

2 Tbsp. coconut oil, melted

¾ c. almond milk

¼ c. coconut sugar

1½ tsp. vanilla extract

1 c. carrots, grated and packed into the cup

¼ c. shredded coconut

¼ c. walnuts, chopped

¼ c. raisins

Instructions

1. Preheat the oven to 425° F. Lightly grease a muffin pan.

2. In a small bowl, whisk together the flax meal and the warm water. Set aside for a few minutes to thicken.

3. Use a food processor to whirl the rolled oats into oat flour and then put them in a large mixing bowl. Add the baking powder, cinnamon, baking soda, nutmeg, ginger, and salt and mix until combined.

4. Add the flax seed mixture into a bowl with the applesauce, coconut oil, almond milk, sugar, and vanilla. Make a well in the middle of the dry ingredients and add the wet ingredients. Mix just until the batter is not dry.

5. Fold in the carrots, coconut, walnuts, and raisins and stir just until combined.

6. Pour the batter into the muffin cups, only filling about 2/3- ¾ full. Bake for 5 minutes at 425°F, and then lower the temperature to 375°F and bake for 20-22 minutes, until a fork inserted in the middle is clean.

Makes 12 muffins

PB&J Smoothies

You can easily adapt this smoothie for any flavors you prefer. I love that it's packed with nutrient dense ingredients.

PB&J Smoothies

Ingredients

- 1 c. rolled oats
- ¼ c. natural peanut butter
- 1-2 frozen bananas
- 1 c. almond milk
- 1 c. frozen strawberries (or raspberries, cherries, other red fruit)
- 1 Tbsp. chia seeds, flax seeds, or other nuts/seeds chopped

Instructions

1. Blend all the ingredients in a high-speed blender until smooth and thick. You can add more oats if the mixture seems too thin or use more almond milk to thin it out.

Serves 2-3

Kale Salad with Lentils and Butternut Squash

Massaging kale makes it easier for all ages to eat. This salad is a complete meal with tons of calcium and protein.

Kale Salad with Lentils and Butternut Squash

Ingredients

1 butternut squash, peeled chopped into small chunks

2 Tbsp. coconut oil

pinch of salt

1 head of kale, washed and chopped

1 15 oz. can of lentils (or use freshly cooked lentils)

¼ c. balsamic vinegar

1 garlic clove, minced (or use ½ tsp. garlic powder)

1 Tbsp. Dijon mustard

1 Tbsp. maple syrup

½ tsp. dried parsley

½ tsp. dried basil

½ tsp. dried oregano

¼ tsp. salt

2 Tbsp. extra virgin olive oil

½ c. pomegranate or unsweetened dried cranberries, optional

Instructions

1. Preheat the oven to 400°F. Place the chopped butternut squash onto a baking sheet and cover with coconut oil and salt, making sure it has covered the squash. Bake for about 25-30 minutes, until the squash is tender but not falling apart.

2. Massage the kale with a splash of olive oil to break down the fibers and then place the kale in a large serving bowl. Top with the lentils and butternut squash and then cover the kale with them.

3. Combine the vinegar, garlic, mustard, maple syrup, and herbs in a small bowl. Drizzle in the olive oil while whisking the dressing to emulsify the ingredients. Top the salad with the dressing, and sprinkle on pomegranate or cranberries to finish.

Serves 4

Greek Salad with Tofu Feta

Greek salad is a perfect compliment to a soup or sandwich. We had fun assembling this salad together.

Greek Salad with Tofu Feta

Ingredients

1 head of romaine lettuce, chopped

1 large cucumber, sliced

4 medium tomatoes, chopped

½ c. Kalamata olives

¼ c. red wine vinegar

1 garlic clove, minced

Optional Marinade for Feta

1 tsp. lemon juice

1 Tbsp. apple cider vinegar

1 Tbsp. olive oil

3 Tbsp. water

1 Tbsp. Dijon mustard

1 Tbsp. maple syrup

½ tsp. dried oregano

¼ tsp. salt (or omit for under 1

year old)

2 Tbsp. extra virgin olive oil

1 package extra firm tofu, cut into bite size pieces

2 Tbsp. nutritional yeast

1 Tbsp. dried oregano

½ tsp. salt

black pepper

Instructions

1. Combine the lettuce, cucumber, tomatoes, and olives in a big salad bowl and set aside. You can top with chunks of tofu, either plain, roasted, the precooked and marinated kind from the grocery store, or try making these marinated feta chunks.

2. To make the red wine vinaigrette, combine the vinegar, garlic, mustard, maple syrup, and herbs in a small bowl. Drizzle in the olive oil while whisking the dressing to emulsify the ingredients.

3. To make the tofu feta, whisk together all of the ingredients and place it into an airtight container with the pieces of tofu. Shake it up to make sure every piece of tofu gets the marinade on it, and let it sit for at least 2 hours. You can let it marinate for a few days.

Serves 4

Raw Kale Salad with Garlic Tahini Dressing

The key to serving anyone raw kale is to massage the leaves until you can't hear the fibers snapping anymore. It's easier to chew and to digest.

Raw Kale Salad with Garlic Tahini Dressing

Ingredients

1 bunch of kale, washed and cut into small pieces

1 Tbsp. olive oil

1 garlic clove, grated

¼ c. tahini

2 Tbsp. apple cider vinegar

2 Tbsp. liquid aminos

2 Tbsp. nutritional yeast

¼- ½ c. water, depending on how thin you like it

Instructions

1. After you've cut the kale on the cutting board, sprinkle olive oil over the kale.

2. Use your hands to massage the kale, squeezing the olive into the leaves repeatedly until you don't feel or hear any more popping. What you're doing is breaking down the fibers of the leaves so the kale is soft and easy to chew.

3. Whisk the rest of the ingredients together until blended and then top the kale with the dressing.

Serves 2-4

Chickpea Salad

We eat chickpea salad on sandwiches, in salads, as an accompaniment to grains and greens, and on its own. The kelp is what gives it that oceany flavor so you can add more or less.

Chickpea Salad

Ingredients

1 stalk celery

¼ c. red onion

1 15 oz. can of chickpeas, drained

2 Tbsp. lemon juice

2 Tbsp. vegan mayonnaise

1 Tbsp. capers

1 Tbsp. chopped pickles or relish

2 Tbsp. pickles

1 tsp. Dijon mustard

1 tsp. kelp powder

pinch of salt and pepper

Instructions

1. Combine the celery and onion in a food processor and pulse until it breaks into small pieces.

2. Add in the remaining ingredients and pulse just until the chickpeas are smashed, not smooth like hummus.

Serves 2-4

Potato Salad

I adore making potato salad, and typically use a lemon vinaigrette like this one rather than a mayonnaise-based dressing. The two flavors go perfectly together.

Potato Salad

Ingredients

1 pound fingerling potatoes, chopped (Red Potatoes or Yukon gold also work)

pinch of salt

1 celery stalk, diced

1 Tbsp. capers

3 Tbsp. fresh lemon juice, about 1-2 lemons

1 Tbsp. Dijon mustard

1 garlic clove, minced (or use ½ tsp. garlic powder)

2 tsp. dried dill

pinch of salt and pepper (to taste)

2 Tbsp. extra virgin olive oil

Instructions

1. Steam the potatoes until tender but not falling apart. This typically takes about 20 minutes, but it depends on the type of potatoes and the size you cut, so just watch them. When they're done steaming I like to salt them right away, but if you have a baby under 1 you can omit this step here and just salt at the table.

2. Add the potatoes to a large bowl with the celery and capers, and then dress with the lemon dill dressing.

3. Whisk the lemon juice, mustard, garlic, dill, and salt together. Then whisk the dressing while drizzling in the olive oil to combine the ingredients.

Serves 2-4

Eggy Tofu Salad

Here's another throwback sandwich filling that gets its signature flavor from black salt. You can find black salt in many health food stores and international markets. It's actually pink, and has a strong sulfur flavor that makes food taste like eggs.

Eggy Tofu Salad

Ingredients

1 green onion

1 stalk celery

1 16 oz. package of firm tofu

1 Tbsp. vegan mayonnaise

½ tsp. black salt (If you can't find it, you can sub in regular salt here)

½ tsp. turmeric

Instructions

1. Combine the green onion and celery in a food processor and pulse until you have small pieces.

2. Add in the remaining ingredients and pulse until combined, but not smooth. You want small chunks of tofu to remain.

Serves 2-4

Classic Veggie Gumbo

I went to school in New Orleans and so gumbo has always held a special place in my heart. When okra pops up at the farmers market, it's the first thing that comes to mind. My daughter has always loved this stew. You can use vegan sausage to make it even more authentic, or it's great just with chickpeas.

Classic Veggie Gumbo

Ingredients

3 Tbsp. olive oil

¼ c. all-purpose flour

1 medium onion, diced

1 tsp. salt (omit for < 1 yr)

3 garlic cloves, minced

1 red bell pepper, diced

1 15 oz. can tomatoes

fresh black pepper

2 bay leaf

1 tsp. smoked paprika

1 tsp. dried thyme

3 c. vegetable broth

2 c. okra, sliced

1 15 oz. can kidney beans

1 15 oz. can chickpeas

1 Tbsp. fresh lemon juice

Instructions

1. I like to serve gumbo with brown rice, so I start cooking that before the gumbo, so it's ready at the end. I use 1½ parts water to 1 part brown rice, and use 1 cup dried rice for 3-4 people, which yields 3 cups cooked.

2. In a large soup pot, combined the olive oil and flour and stir with a wooden spoon. Stir for about 3-5 minutes, until the flour smells toasty and the mixture is light brown. It will be clumpy, which is perfect. Add the onions and salt and stir to coat the onions in the flour mixture. Cook for about 5 minutes, stirring frequently. Add in the garlic and cook for another 30 seconds.

3. Add the peppers and tomatoes and cook for 10 minutes. Add in the pepper, bay leaves, paprika, thyme, and slowly add in the vegetable broth, stirring around the pot to prevent lumps from forming. Add in the okra and the beans and bring the soup up to a boil. Cover and reduce the heat to a simmer, cooking for about 30- 45 minutes. The gumbo will thicken up and the okra will soften and it will taste marvelous.

4. Remove the bay leaf and stir in the lemon juice.

Serves 4-6

Potato Leek Soup

Leeks? Yes! My children love them. It's similar to onion soup and hearty from the coconut milk. This is a messy meal, beware!

Potato Leek Soup

Ingredients

2 Tbsp. olive oil

1 small onion, diced

3 large leeks, cleaned thoroughly (take them apart) and sliced thinly. Just keep the white and light green parts

2 garlic cloves, minced

5 russet potatoes, chopped

1 tsp. salt (omit for < 1)

1 tsp. dried thyme

½ tsp. dried rosemary

5 c. low-sodium vegetable broth

1 bay leaf

1 c. coconut milk

1 Tbsp. fresh lemon juice

Instructions

1. In a large soup pot, combine the olive oil, onions, leeks, and a pinch of salt. Cook for about 5 minutes, until the vegetables have softened. Add in the garlic and cook for another 30 seconds.

2. Add in the potatoes, salt, thyme, and rosemary and stir for a minute, then add in the vegetable broth and the bay leaf. Cover and bring to a boil and then lower the heat to a simmer. Cook for about 30 minutes, until the potatoes are tender. Remove the pot from the heat and add in the coconut milk and lemon juice. 3. Take out the bay leaf and compost it.

3. At this point you can use an immersion blender to make the soup nice and creamy, or you can transfer it to a blender instead. You'd have to do it in batches, which means extra bowls to wash, so I prefer to just use my immersion blender.

Serves 4-6

Broccoli Cheddar Soup

Healthier and heartier than its original non-vegan counterpart. You can thicken this soup like in this picture or loosen it with more broth.

Broccoli Cheddar Soup

Ingredients

1 Tbsp. olive oil

5 c. low-sodium

1 yellow onion, diced

3 garlic cloves, minced

4 c. broccoli, chopped (about one medium)

1 carrot, chopped

½ tsp. ground turmeric

4 c. vegetable broth, divided

1 c. cashews

3 Tbsp. mellow miso

3 Tbsp. nutritional yeast

2 Tbsp. fresh lemon juice

Instructions

1. Heat the olive oil and onion with a pinch of salt over medium heat in a large soup pot. Cook for about 5 minutes, and then add in the garlic and cook for another 30 seconds.

2. Add the broccoli, carrots, turmeric, and half of the vegetable broth. Bring the soup to a boil and then cover and reduce the heat to low. Cook for another 10-15 minutes until the vegetables are soft.

3. Meanwhile, combine the cashews, remaining half of vegetable broth, miso, and nutritional yeast in the blender. Whirl until it's smooth, from 2-5 minutes depending on your blender. As a side note, if you don't have a strong blender like a Vitamix, you should plan to soak your cashews overnight in water and then drain them before blending into this recipe.

4. When the vegetables are soft in the pot, add them into the blender and pulse until there are fine bits of broccoli, but not until they are completely smooth. Or, you can add the cashew mixture into the soup pot and use an immersion blender to break the broccoli and carrots up. Let the soup cook for another 10 minutes. Remove from the heat and add lemon juice.

Serves 4-6

Mediterranean Vegetable Soup

I love making vegetable soups with these Mediterranean spices. The key to good soup is giving the aromatics of onion, garlic, carrots, and celery time to soften and flavor the base of the soup.

Mediterranean Vegetable Soup

Ingredients

1 onion, chopped

1 Tbsp. olive oil

2 garlic clove, minced

1 large carrot, peeled and sliced in circles

1 stalk celery, sliced in semi-circles

2-3 Yukon gold potatoes, diced

1 tsp. basil

1 tsp. oregano

1 tsp. thyme

1 tsp. salt (omit for under 1 year old)

freshly ground black pepper

6 c. vegetable broth

1 32 oz. can tomato puree

1 15 oz. can chickpeas

1 15 oz. can kidney beans

Instructions

1. Heat the onion and the olive oil with a pinch of salt in a large soup pot over medium heat until the onions are translucent, about 5 minutes. Add in the garlic and cook for just about 30 seconds. Add in the carrots and celery and another pinch of salt. Cook the vegetables until just softened, about 3-4 minutes. Add in the potatoes, the basil, oregano, thyme, and salt and stir to combine.

2. Add in the vegetable broth and scrape the bottom of the pot to make sure you loosen any charred onions pieces. Bring the broth to a boil and then lower the heat to medium-low, cooking just until the potatoes soften, about 10 minutes. Add in the tomato puree and beans and cook for another 10 minutes on low heat. Taste for salt and pepper.

Serves 4-6

Black Bean Soup

The first time my daughter looked at black bean soup she refused to eat it, I think because it's dark brown. I asked if she wanted to take just one taste and she said, "mmmm," and then she gobbled it up.

Black Bean Soup

Ingredients

2 Tbsp. olive oil

1 large medium onion, chopped

3 celery stalks, chopped

1 large carrot, chopped

6 garlic cloves, minced

1 Tbsp. cumin

2 tsp. dried oregano

1 tsp. dried thyme

4 15 oz. cans black beans, drained (or soaked and cooked beans)

4 c. low-sodium vegetable broth

2 Tbsp. fresh lime juice

Instructions

1. Heat the olive oil with the onion, celery, and carrots with a pinch of salt in a large soup pan over medium heat.

2. Cook for about 10 minutes, until the vegetables are tender. Stir in the garlic and cumin, oregano, and thyme and cook for about 30 seconds.

3. Add in the beans and vegetable broth and bring to a boil over high heat, and then reduce to low.

4. Simmer for about 30 minutes until it's flavorful and fragrant. I like to smash some of the beans as I'm cooking so it's nice and creamy. When it's done cooking, add in the lime juice and serve.

Serves 4-6

Lentil Vegetable Soup

Lentils are the much maligned vegan food that really don't deserve to be treated so badly. When you cook them well they have a nice bite and can absorb so many flavors. Tarragon is the secret star ingredient.

Lentil Vegetable Soup

Ingredients

1 onion, chopped

1 Tbsp. olive oil

2 garlic cloves, minced

1 large carrot, peeled and diced

1 stalk of celery, diced

1 tsp. thyme

1 tsp. tarragon

1 c. French lentils

1 tsp. salt (omit for under 1 year old)

freshly ground black pepper

6 c. vegetable broth

1 32 oz. can of tomato puree

Instructions

1. Heat the onions, carrots, and celery and the olive oil with a pinch of salt in a large soup pot over medium heat until the onions are translucent, about 5 minutes.

2. Add in the garlic and cook for just about 30 seconds. Cook the vegetables until just softened, about 3-4 minutes. Add in the thyme, tarragon, and lentils and cook for a few minutes.

3. Add in the vegetable broth and tomatoes and scrape the bottom of the pot to make sure you loosen any charred onions pieces.

4. Bring the broth to a boil and then lower the heat to medium-low, cooking until the lentils are soft enough to bite but not falling apart. Taste for salt and pepper.

Serves 4-6

Curried Butternut Squash Soup

There's a strong undercurrent of coconut in this soup and it gives a lush creaminess to the texture to the soup. Kids love it.

Curried Butternut Squash Soup

Ingredients

1 Tbsp. coconut oil

1 medium onion, diced

2 garlic cloves, minced

1 medium butternut squash, cut into chunks

salt and freshly ground black pepper (omit for under 1 year old)

1 tsp. curry powder

¼ tsp. ground cinnamon

1 14 oz. can coconut milk

2 c. vegetable broth

2 Tbsp. maple syrup (or sub coconut sugar)

Instructions

1. In a large soup pot over medium heat, heat the oil and onions with a pinch of salt, until the onions are translucent, about 5 minutes. Add in the garlic and sauté for about 1 minute.

2. Add butternut squash with a pinch each salt and pepper, curry powder, and ground cinnamon. Stir to coat, then cover and cook for 4 minutes, stirring occasionally.

3. Add coconut milk, vegetable broth, maple syrup or coconut sugar. Bring to a low boil over medium heat and then reduce heat to low, cover, and simmer for 15 minutes, or until butternut squash is fork tender.

4. Transfer the soup to a blender (or use an immersion blender) and puree until the soup is smooth. Return the soup to the pot and cook for a few more minutes over medium heat. Taste for salt or sweetener.

Serves 4-6

Split Pea Soup

Split pea soup is another hearty favorite in my house and it's a great soup to start babies with. It's another than can be thickened or loosened easily depending on the amount of broth you add.

Split Pea Soup

Ingredients

1-2 Tbsp. olive oil

1 medium onion, chopped

4 stalks celery, chopped

3 large carrots, chopped

4 garlic cloves, minced

1 bay leaf

1 tsp. coriander

1 tsp. basil

1 tsp. thyme

1 tsp. parsley

1.5 tsp. salt

1/2 c. barley

black pepper, to taste

2 c. split peas, sorted and rinsed

6-8 c. water or vegetable broth

1 Tbsp. brown miso

1 tsp. liquid smoke (optional)

Instructions

1. In a large soup pot, heat the olive oil over medium heat and add the onion, cooking until translucent, about 10 minutes.

2. Add celery, carrots, and garlic and cook for another 2-3 minutes, until fragrant.

3. Add bay leaf, coriander, basil, thyme, parsley, salt, barley, split peas, and stock. Bring to a boil, cover, and then reduce temperature to low. Simmer for 1-2 hours, until the peas are soft.

4. Taste and add miso and smoke, to taste. Remove the bay leaf.

5. Using an immersion blender (or pouring everything into a blender), blend until smooth and creamy, or to the texture you like.

6. Makes about 8-10 servings. The flavors meld and this vegan soup recipe tastes even better the day after cooking.

Serves 4-6

Minestrone Soup

Minestrone has a slight variation from a typical vegetable soup, with more added beans and different herbs. This is a family favorite.

Minestrone Soup

Ingredients

1 onion, chopped

1 Tbsp. olive oil

2 garlic cloves, minced

1 large carrot, sliced

1 stalk celery, sliced

1 large zucchini, sliced

2-3 gold potatoes, diced

1 bay leaf

1 tsp. oregano

1 tsp. thyme

½ tsp. rosemary

1 tsp. salt (omit for <1)

ground black pepper

6 c. vegetable broth

1 32 oz. can tomato puree

1 15 oz. can kidney beans

1 15 oz. can cannellini beans

1 c. green beans, cut in 1"

1 bunch of kale, chopped

½ box whole wheat shells

Instructions

1. Heat the onion and the olive oil with a pinch of salt in a large soup pot over medium heat until the onions are translucent, about 5 minutes. Add the garlic and cook for just about 30 seconds, then add the carrots and celery and a pinch of salt. Cook the vegetables until just softened, about 3-4 minutes. Add in the potatoes, the bay leaf, oregano, thyme, and salt and stir to combine.

2. Add the broth and scrape the bottom of the pot to make sure you loosen any charred onions pieces. Bring the soup to a boil and lower to medium-low, cooking just until the potatoes soften, about 10 minutes.

3. Add the tomato puree, beans, and green beans and cook for 10 minutes on low heat. At the end, add the kale and remove the bay leaf. Taste for seasoning.

4. I like to cook the pasta shells separately and then add them when I serve the soup. You can just add them when you add the tomato puree and beans if you want to make the whole process faster.
Serves 4- 6

Roasted Cauliflower Steaks

Cutting the cauliflower like a slice of bread allows so many more planes to brown when you roast it, giving the vegetable a sweetness and crunchy texture that's hard to otherwise achieve.

Roasted Cauliflower Steaks

Ingredients

1 large head cauliflower

1-2 Tbsp. olive oil

pinch of salt and pepper (omit for under 1 year olds)

Instructions

1. Preheat the oven to 400° F.

2. Hold the head of cauliflower sideways in your hand and slice through the entire thing like you're slicing bread. Make slices about every ¾ inch so you have large slices of the entire head of cauliflower.

3. Lay the cauliflower steaks flat on a baking sheet and sprinkle olive oil, salt and pepper over everything and then rub it in with your hands.

4. Bake for 30-45 minutes until the tops and edges of the cauliflower are brown and crunchy, flipping once midway through.

Serves 2-3

Garlic Sauteéd Broccoli

This is a super flavorful and simple way to prepare broccoli. One saucepan, a handful of minced garlic, and some chopped broccoli.

Garlic Sautéed Broccoli

Ingredients

2 heads broccoli

2-3 garlic cloves, minced

2-3 Tbsp. olive oil

Pinch of salt and pepper

Instructions

1. Slice the broccoli into very small florets, so that there are plenty of tiny bits of broccoli on your cutting board. This is the key difference with this recipe—the tiny pieces of broccoli that all absorb the garlic oil flavor.

2. In a large saucepan over medium heat, heat the olive oil, garlic, and salt and pepper until the garlic is just barely starting to turn golden brown.

3. Add in the broccoli and toss to coat, stirring well. Cook until the broccoli softens, about 5-7 minutes, stirring often. It's great if some of the pieces start to turn crispy and brown.

Serves 4-6

Roasted Sweet Potato Wedges

My daughter loves sweet potatoes, and this is one of her favorite ways to eat them. The lime and garlic give them immense Caribbean flavor, and the texture is perfect for beginning eaters.

Roasted Sweet Potato Wedges

Ingredients

3 sweet potatoes

2 Tbsp. olive oil

pinch of salt (omit for under 1 year old)

2 Tbsp. freshly squeezed lime juice

2 big garlic cloves, minced or grated

Instructions

1. Preheat the oven to 400° F.

2. Cut the sweet potatoes lengthwise into thick wedges. Cover with olive oil and salt and lay flat on a baking sheet. Bake for 30-45 minutes, until the sweet potatoes are soft.

3. While the sweet potatoes are baking, mix the lime juice and garlic in a shallow dish.

4. When you remove them from the oven, gently place them in the dish and toss with the dressing to coat. They're delicious served warm but we also eat them cold as leftovers.

Serves 4-6

Classic Baked Potatoes

This may seem like an overly simple recipe, but I was actually always just winging it until I learned how to make perfect baked potatoes every single time. Covered with oozy cheese sauce with a side of vegetables and some baked beans it's a full meal.

Classic Baked Potatoes

Ingredients

1 baked potato per person

olive oil to coat

salt and pepper (omit for under 1 years old)

Instructions

1. Preheat the oven to 350° F. Poke holes in the baked potatoes so they don't explode in the oven.

2. Rub olive oil over each baked potato and sprinkle with salt and pepper.

3. Place in the middle rack of the oven and bake for 60 minutes, until the potatoes are soft.

4. Cut them open and fill with vegan cheese, sour cream, green onions, chili, beans, olive oil, or just eat totally plain!

Serves 4-6

Baked Zucchini with Parmesan

My mom used to bake zucchini with parmesan all the time when I was a kid and I found a perfect way to recreate the flavor and texture with this simple cheesy topping.

Baked Zucchini with Parmesan

Ingredients

3 large zucchini, cut into half lengthwise

olive oil to coat

salt and pepper (omit if under 1 years old)

2 Tbsp. almond meal

2 Tbsp. nutritional yeast

½ tsp. salt (omit if under 1 years old)

Instructions

1. Preheat the oven to 350° F.

2. Coat the zucchini with olive oil and salt and place them flat on a baking sheet. Bake for 30 minutes, until soft but still firm enough to pick up.

3. In a small bowl combine the almond meal, nutritional yeast, and salt. Sprinkle the almond cheese mixture over the zucchini.

Serves 4-6

Garlic Green Beans

It can't get much easier than steamed green beans tossed in garlic and olive oil, and kids absolutely love this vegetable side dish.

Garlic Green Beans

Ingredients

1 pound organic green beans

2 Tbsp. organic extra virgin olive oil

1 garlic clove, grated

¼ tsp. salt (leave out before 1 year old)

Instructions

1. Steam the green beans until they are soft but still have some crunch. For under one year old, I steam until there's not much crunch and just enough firmness so your child can hold onto the bean without squishing it.

2. In a large bowl stir together the olive oil, the garlic, and the salt.

3. When the green beans are done, run them under cold water and then blot them dry with a clean dishtowel.

4. Gently fold the green beans into the olive oil, making sure there's oil on each green bean.

Serves 4-6

Sautéed Spring Snap Peas

I love fresh green peas and snap peas in the springtime, and adding some lightly cooked green onions and garlic goes perfectly with them.

Sautéed Spring Snap Peas

Ingredients

¼ c. green onions, chopped

1 garlic clove, minced

2 Tbsp. olive oil

1 lb. sugar snap peas, rinsed

pinch of salt

Instructions

1. Cook the green onions and garlic with the olive oil in a saucepan over medium heat, until fragrant and translucent and slightly browned.

2. Add in the snap peas and salt and toss to cover them with the onions mixture.

3. Allow to cook just until they start to look bright green, but don't overcook them! They should still have a ton of crunch. I like to see them turn slightly translucent around the edges and then turn off the heat.

Serves 4-6

Black Rice and Beet Salad

Black rice is fun because it's different, and it also has a light sweetness to it that makes it appealing for kids. If you can't find it, any rice will be perfect in this dish. Just keep in mind that the beets will color everything pinkish.

Ingredients

5-6 large beets, peeled and cut into a large dice

1 c. black rice (or rice, quinoa, etc.), rinsed

1½ c. water

¼ c. apple cider vinegar

2 Tbsp. Dijon mustard

1 Tbsp. maple syrup

1-2 garlic cloves, grated

1 tsp. dried thyme

½ tsp. sea salt

¼ c. olive oil

½ c. pecans

1 head kale, chopped into small pieces

2 tomatoes, diced

Instructions

1. Preheat the oven to 400° F. Put the diced beets on a baking sheet and cover with a tablespoon of olive oil and a pinch of salt. Mix the beets around to make sure the olive oil covers all the beets, and then bake for about 30-40 minutes, stirring a few times, until the beets are soft and slightly crunchy.

Black Rice and Beet Salad

2. While the beets are roasting, bring the water and rice to a boil in a small pot, and then reduce the heat to a simmer. Cook the rice for about 30-40 minutes, until the water is absorbed and the rice is tender. Don't stir it during the cooking time. You can use a fork to gently pull aside a section of rice to see if all the water is gone, and if it happens to be gone and the rice isn't cooked, add a little more water and continue cooking

3. In a large serving bowl, combine the vinegar, mustard, maple syrup, garlic, thyme, and salt. Continue whisking while slowly pouring in the olive oil. This will help to emulsify the dressing so it doesn't separate.

4. Sprinkle a little olive oil on your chopped kale and massage it into the leaves, breaking down the fibers and making the kale nice and soft. When you can't hear any more crackling when you are massaging, add the kale into the serving bowl with the dressing.

5. To this bowl you'll also add the cooked beets and rice when both are finished, and then top with the pecans and tomatoes. Stir it all together and let it sit in the refrigerator for a few hours to absorb all the flavors.

Serves 4-6

Crunchy Persian Rice with Chickpeas

One of my best friends is Persian and I have to say, my version of this doesn't come close to hers because she has been making this dish for 30 years. Even still, it's delicious. (Imagine what hers tastes like, right?) The crunchy rice is fun and highly requested around here, and these chickpeas are incredible. It might look difficult because of how much I've written about making it, but it's really easy.

Ingredients

1½ c. water

1 c. basmati rice, rinsed thoroughly, drained

4 Tbsp. olive oil for rice

2 Tbsp. olive oil for the chickpeas

1 tsp. ground cumin

1 onion, chopped

1 garlic clove, chopped

½" piece of ginger, grated

1 tsp. salt (omit for under 1-year-olds)

ground black pepper

juice from 1 lime

1 Tbsp. tomato paste

1 15 oz. can of chickpeas, drained and rinsed

1 tomato, diced

2 tsp. dried basil

Crunchy Persian Rice with Chickpeas

Instructions

1. Begin making the rice by bringing the water to a boil in a small saucepan. Add the rice and stir once, then bring the water up to a boil. When it reaches a boil, lower the heat to low and cover.

2. After 15 minutes, if you gently push a knife on the side of the rice, you should see that the water is almost gone, but still remaining. If you touch a piece of rice, it will taste soft but still firm and uncooked. At this point you should drizzle the olive oil evenly across the top of the rice. The oil will sink to the bottom and help to create a crust on the rice.

3. Put the lid back on the pan and cook until all the water is absorbed, about 10-15 more minutes. (If you use brown basmati rice the whole thing will take longer to cook, about 50 minutes total.) Taste a piece of rice from the top and it should be fully cooked. I wait until I can hear crackling to be sure there's a nice crust forming on the bottom layer of the pan. Then remove it from the heat and give it about 15 minutes to rest.

4. To present like a true Persian, you'll want to flip this rice over and have the crunchy part rest on the top of the rest of rice, like a flan. I have to reiterate here that I wasn't raised watching anyone make this so I don't have a ton of experience with it. Most of the time part of mine falls or breaks apart, and I often have to scrape rice from the bottom of the pan. It doesn't matter at all to me that it doesn't look perfect. It tastes awesome, and my daughter loves the crunchy texture.

5. What I do is put a plate on top of the saucepan and then, using an oven mitt, flip the saucepan over to invert the rice. If you are wonderful, it will all plop out in one piece. Otherwise, scrape the bottom!

6. While the rice is cooking, make the chickpeas. Heat the olive oil in a large skillet over medium heat. Add the cumin and toast it for 1 minute. Add in the onion, garlic, ginger, salt, and pepper and cook for about 5 minutes. Then add in the lime juice and tomato paste and cook for another 5 minutes.

7. Add in the chickpeas, tomato, and basil and cook until heated through. Serve with olive oil and crunchy rice.

Serves 4-6

Beans, Grains, and Greens

This is my go-to dish for any meal where I'm busy and I've run out of time to be creative or I just don't want to follow a recipe. You can adapt it any way you like based on what grains you have at home, what vegetables are in season, and what canned or frozen beans are in your fridge. If you have time to tie it all together with a nice sauce (check out the dips and dressings section), that's a plus, but my daughter loves this as is with olive oil and nutritional yeast or a pinch of salt.

Beans, Grains, and Greens

Ingredients

2 c. water

1 c. dried whole grains (rice, quinoa, millet, farro, freekah, etc.)

1 Tbsp. olive oil

1 garlic clove, minced

1 bunch of kale, rinsed and chopped (or chard, spinach, etc.)

1 pinch of nutmeg, optional

1 pinch salt (omit for under 1 year olds)

1 more Tbsp. olive oil

1 more clove of garlic, minced

1 15 oz. can beans (or 2 c. cooked beans)

½ tsp. cumin

½ tsp. oregano

Instructions

1. Bring the water to a boil in a small saucepan. Add in the grains and stir gently, then bring it back to a boil. Lower the heat to low and cover, cooking until the water is absorbed and the grains are soft. Don't stir! (There are different cooking times for each type of whole grain.)

2. In a large saucepan, heat up 1 tablespoon of oil. Add in 1 tablespoon of minced garlic and cook just for about 30 seconds, until the garlic is fragrant and just slightly browned. Don't let it burn or it gets bitter. Drop in the kale, nutmeg, and salt, and stir to coat with olive oil and garlic. Cook just until the greens start to wilt, and then remove them from the pan.

3. In the same saucepan, heat another tablespoon of oil. Add in the second tablespoon of minced garlic and cook just for 30 seconds, until the garlic is fragrant. Add in the beans and herbs and cook until heated thoroughly. Serve.

Serves 4-6

Spaghetti with Bean Balls

Okay, this isn't a picture of the bean balls, but they'd be perfect on this spaghetti dish. See the tempeh balls picture for a photo of the balls.

Spaghetti with Bean Balls

Ingredients

2 8 oz. packages tempeh

1 Tbsp. low-sodium soy sauce or Bragg's Aminos

1 Tbsp. olive oil

1 small onion, diced

3 garlic clove, minced

3 Tbsp. ketchup

2 tsp. Dijon mustard

1 tsp. dried oregano

1 tsp. dried thyme, crumbled

1 tsp. dried sage

½ tsp. salt

1 c. breadcrumbs

olive oil for cooking

1 package spaghetti

1 batch spaghetti sauce (pg. 18)

Instructions

1. Crumble the tempeh into a steamer basket and steam for about 10 minutes, until the tempeh is soft. Remove from the heat and sprinkle on the Bragg's liquid aminos and then let the tempeh cool. In a saucepan, cook the olive oil and onions with a pinch of salt until translucent, about 5 minutes. Add in the garlic and cook for another 30 seconds. Remove the onions from the heat and put them into a large mixing bowl.

2. Add the tempeh, the ketchup, mustard, oregano, thyme, sage, and salt to the mixing bowl and stir until combined. Add in the breadcrumbs and stir well. You should be able to pick up the mixture and easily form balls, but if the mixture is crumbly, you can add more breadcrumbs, a tablespoon at a time.

3. Roll the tempeh mixture into tight balls about the size of golf balls. Cook them in a large saucepan with a tablespoon of olive oil, turning after about 5 minutes on each side until you have browned each side.

4. Remove from the heat and serve warm. You can also freeze them at this stage and reheat them later.

Serves 4-6

Mac-N-Cheese with Broccoli

I like stuffing this classic kids dish with as many vegetables as I can. What's great is that the potatoes and cashews blend together to give it a creamy, gooey texture that everyone will love, even kids who are switching over to a vegan diet and are used to "real" mac-n-cheese.

Ingredients

1 head of broccoli, washed and trimmed into nice holding pieces

3 medium Yukon gold or red potatoes

3" chunk of sweet potato

½ small red pepper

2 medium carrots

¼ of an onion

3 garlic cloves, peeled

1 tsp. olive oil

½ c. cashews

1 tsp. fresh lemon juice (or use half a lemon in the blender)

1 tsp. chickpea miso

1 tsp. prepared mustard

1 tsp. sea salt (omit for children under 1 year old)

1 box whole wheat elbow macaroni

Mac-N-Cheese with Broccoli

Instructions

1. You can plan to either mix your broccoli in with the macaroni or serve it on the side. If you want to add it into the macaroni, I recommend chopping it and then steaming it. Steam the broccoli for a few minutes until it's soft, but not overcooked.

2. In the meantime, fill a saucepot with water and bring to a boil with the potatoes, sweet potato, pepper, carrots, and onion. When the vegetables are tender, about 20-25 minutes later, remove them from the water. You might want to save some water to thin out the sauce later if it gets too thick, so I don't drain it yet.

3. While the vegetables are cooking, roast the garlic with the olive oil for a few minutes until it's fragrant and light brown. I put it in my toaster oven on 400 degrees for about 10 minutes, watch to see it doesn't burn.

4. Put the cooked vegetables, roasted garlic, cashews, lemon (or lemon juice), miso, mustard, and salt into a high-speed blender and blend until the mixture is smooth and creamy. Thin with cooking water if needed.

5. Note: If you don't have a powerful blender, I would go slowly with this, starting with the potatoes, then add the other cooked vegetables and garlic, add the cashews next, and then add the remaining ingredients.

6. Cook the macaroni according to the directions and then top it with the sauce and broccoli and serve. Note: I've always been a lover of wet mac-n-cheese, finding its texture nicer than the baked version. If you like a nice thick, gooey mac-n-cheese, feel free to bake it here for about 30 minutes on 350 degrees F. Bread crumbs and olive oil on top will help it to get nice and crusty.

Serves 4 - 6

Fettuccine Alfredo with Shiitake Bacon

It's crazy how the shiitakes cook up into the same crispy, crunch texture as bacon. They don't even really need much flavoring to be convincing; just a thin slice and some sea salt.

Fettuccine Alfredo with Shiitake Bacon

Ingredients

1 lb. shiitake mushrooms, washed and sliced thinly (creminis work too)

1 Tbsp. olive oil

1 onion, chopped

2 garlic cloves, chopped

1½ c. raw cashews

2 c. water

1 Tbsp. lemon juice

1 tsp. sea salt (omit for children under 1)

1 lb. whole grain fettuccine noodles

Instructions

1. Preheat the oven to 350 degrees F. Place the sliced mushrooms on a baking sheet and cover with a splash of olive oil and a sprinkle of salt, making sure each piece is covered with oil. Bake until crispy, about 30 minutes.

2. To prepare the Alfredo sauce, heat the tablespoon of olive oil and the onion in a saucepan with a p of salt. Cook until the onions are translucent, about 5 minutes. Add the garlic and cook for 30 seconds, then remove from the heat.

3. Add the onions and garlic to the rest of the ingredients in a blender and whirl until creamy and smooth. If don't have a super powerful blender, I recommend soaking the cashews overnight in water (drain before adding to the blender), and starting your blender with the cashews and water. Then add the other ingredients.

4. Cook the fettuccine noodles and then return them to the cooking pan and top them with the Alfredo sauce. If the sauce looks a little thin, you can turn the heat back on the pan and cook for a few minutes until it's thickened right on top of the noodles. If it's too thick, add a spoon of water.

5. Top the pasta with your crunchy shiitake mushrooms and serve warm.

Serves 4-6

Chickpeas and Noodles

This is pretty basic, but really tasty. It's perfect when you don't have much time or energy to invest. I make it with all kinds of pasta shapes and add in vegetables for a complete meal in one dish.

Chickpeas and Noodles

Ingredients

½ c. green onion, chopped (about 3-5 stalks)

2 garlic cloves, chopped

2 Tbsp. olive oil

¼ tsp. salt (omit for under 1 years old)

2 Tbsp. nutritional yeast

1 15 oz. can chickpeas, drained

Instructions

1. Bring a saucepan to medium heat. Cook the green onions and garlic in the olive oil until translucent and slightly browned, about 4 minutes.

2. Add in the salt and nutritional yeast and chickpeas, mashing the chickpeas with the back of a spoon or potato masher.

3. Meanwhile, cook the spaghetti until el dente. Transfer the spaghetti to the chickpeas and add in some cooking water until the sauce is smooth and the spaghetti is covered with sauce. Serve warm.

Serves 4-6

Pasta la Caprese

My mom used to make this Italian-influenced pasta salad with a bunch of melty mozzarella cheese. You certainly could add some in, but I have found it's just as good (maybe better!) on its own.

Pasta la Caprese

Ingredients

2-3 yellow banana peppers, julienned (or bell peppers)

5 big ripe tomatoes, julienned (this dish is BEST in the summer when tomatoes are ripe and smell delicious)

4 garlic cloves, crushed and minced

⅓ c. fresh basil, minced

⅓ c. olive oil

salt and pepper, to taste

1 lb. whole grain penne rigate pasta

Instructions

1. Cut the tomatoes and pepper into very tiny strips, julienne style. Crush and mince the garlic and basil.

2. Combine the tomatoes, pepper, garlic, basil, olive oil, salt, and pepper in a large bowl.

3. Cover with plastic wrap and leave on the counter to marinate for several hours. I like to make this around lunch time when I am planning to eat it at dinner because it ripens and livens up over the day. Every time you go in the kitchen it will smell better. It's important not to put this in the fridge (unless it's very hot in the house) because the tomatoes will get mealy.

4. When you are ready to eat, cook the pasta, drain it, and pour over the top. Serve warm.

Serves 4-6

Soba Noodle with Peanut Sauce

We love peanut noodles, and often add in vegetables (the photo has roasted purple cauliflower and sautéed peppers and carrots) to complement the meal.

Soba Noodle with Peanut Sauce

Ingredients

1 12 oz. can coconut milk

¼ c. water

¼ c. maple syrup (you can omit if you don't want any sugar added)

¼ c. liquid aminos or coconut aminos

½ c. natural creamy peanut butter

1 tsp. grated ginger (or use ¼ tsp. dried ginger)

3 garlic cloves, minced or grated

2 Tbsp. lime juice

1 Tbsp. toasted sesame oil

1-2 carrots, shredded

2 green onions, chopped

1 package soba noodles

Instructions

1. Bring a pot of water to a boil and add in the soba noodles. Cook according to the package directions, about 3-5 minutes.

2. Combine all of the ingredients except the lime juice and sesame oil in a saucepan and bring to medium heat.

3. Cook for about 10 minutes, whisking frequently, until everything is combined and the sauce begins to thicken. Remove from the heat and mix in the lime juice and sesame oil.

4. Top the noodles with shredded carrots and onions.

Serves 4-6

Rainbow Tacos

We make many variations on tacos, and this is a nice basic recipe from which to start. One of our favorites is a "rainbow taco," in which I try to put every color of the rainbow. Red peppers, orange sweet potatoes (just bake and then slice), yellow tortillas and onions, green lettuce and peppers, and blue/purple cabbage. I cook the cabbage the same as I do the sliced onions and peppers in this recipe, with olive oil and a touch of salt. You should adjust the amounts of the vegetables based on your family's preferences.

Rainbow Tacos

Ingredients

1 small onion, diced

1 Tbsp. olive oil

2 garlic cloves, chopped

½ tsp. cumin

½ tsp. oregano

salt, to taste

2 15 oz. cans of black beans, drained (or pinto)

1 large onion, sliced

1 Tbsp. olive oil

1-2 green peppers, sliced thinly

½ head lettuce, chopped

3-4 tomatoes, chopped

2 sweet potatoes, baked and sliced

¼ purple cabbage

Corn tortillas

Avocado, sliced

Instructions

1. Heat the olive oil and onion in a saucepan with a pinch of salt. Cook until the onion is translucent, about 5-10 minutes. Add the garlic, cumin, oregano, and salt, and cook for another 30 seconds. Add in the black beans and heat thoroughly, cooking for another 10 minutes or so. Use a potato masher to smash the beans, then stir the mixture until it's creamy.

2. To make the caramelized onions and peppers, add the next batch of sliced onions to a pan with the olive oil and a pinch of salt. Cook them thoroughly, until brown and soft. If the onions start to stick, add a tablespoon of water to deglaze the pan.

3. Remove the onions from the pan and sautee the cabbage with a splash of olive oil and a pinch of salt until it's wilted.

4. To assemble the tacos, I start with a layer of refried beans, cover it with the onions and peppers mix, then layer on lettuce and tomato.

Serves 4-6

Chickpea Patties

Patties are perfect munchers for all aged babies. You can shape these into little logs for tiny hands.

Chickpea Patties

Ingredients

2 15 oz. cans chickpeas, drained

½ c. olive oil

1 c. vegetable broth

½ c. Liquid Amino's or low-sodium soy sauce

3 garlic cloves, minced or grated

2 tsp. lemon zest

2 tsp. dried thyme

1 tsp. sage

½ tsp. paprika

2 c. vital wheat gluten

2 c. breadcrumbs

1 c. all-purpose flour

Instructions

1. Preheat the oven to 350 degrees F.

2. Add the chickpeas and olive oil to a large mixing bowl, and then smash the chickpeas with a potato masher. This takes some arm muscle, so you could use a food processor as an alternative. Just make sure not to blend so thoroughly that you end up with hummus. You want the mixture to be slightly chunky.

3. Add in the vegetable broth, liquid aminos, garlic, zest, thyme, sage, and paprika and stir well. Lastly, add in the wheat gluten, breadcrumbs, flour and stir until the mixture turns into a ball and is very thick.

4. Form the chickpea mixture into balls and then flatten them with your palm, until they are about the size of a burger patty.

5. Assemble the patties in a single layer on a baking sheet and cover with olive oil or cooking spray, making sure the whole thing is covered. Bake for 10-15 minutes on the first side, until it starts to brown and looks solid. Flip and bake for another 5 minutes on the second side.

Serves 4-6

Tempeh Balls

Nice crispy balls for pasta that don't fall apart when you cook them or eat them?! Yes, please! They are also packed with flavor and even omnivores enjoy eating them.

Tempeh Balls

Ingredients

2 8 oz. packages tempeh

1 Tbsp. low-sodium soy sauce or Liquid Aminos

1 Tbsp. olive oil

1 small yellow onion, finely diced

3 garlic cloves, minced

3 Tbsp. ketchup

2 tsp. Dijon mustard

1 tsp. dried oregano

1 tsp. dried thyme, crumbled

1 tsp. dried sage

½ tsp. salt

1 c. whole wheat breadcrumbs

olive oil for cooking the tempeh balls

Instructions

1. Crumble the tempeh into a steamer basket and steam for about 10 minutes, until the tempeh is soft. Remove from the heat and sprinkle on the Bragg's liquid aminos and then let the tempeh cool.

2. In a saucepan, cook the olive oil and onions with a pinch of salt until translucent, about 5 minutes. Add in the garlic and cook for another 30 seconds. Remove the onions and put them into a large mixing bowl.

3. Add the tempeh, the ketchup, mustard, oregano, thyme, sage, and salt to the mixing bowl and stir until combined. Add in the breadcrumbs and stir well. You should be able to pick up the mixture and easily form balls, but if the mixture is crumbly, you can add more breadcrumbs, a tablespoon at a time.

4. Roll the tempeh mixture into tight balls about the size of golf balls. Cook them in a large saucepan with a tablespoon of olive oil, turning after about 5 minutes on each side until you have browned each side. Remove from the heat and serve warm. You can also freeze them at this stage and reheat them later.

Serves 4-6

Zucchini Cakes

The Old Bay seasoning combined with the texture of grated zucchini makes these a dead ringer for crab cakes. My mom, who orders crab cakes in fancy restaurants, always requests these from me when she visits. You'll love the crunchy exterior too.

Zucchini Cakes

Ingredients

4 medium sized zucchini, grated into about 2 cups

1 c. organic whole grain bread crumbs

¼ c. all purpose flour

¼ c. nutritional yeast

¼ red onion, grated

2 Tbsp. coconut oil, melted

1 tsp. Old Bay seasoning (leave out before 1 year old)

salt and pepper to taste (leave out <1 year old)

Olive oil for cooking

Instructions

1. Place the grated zucchini in a clean tea towel and squeeze out as much of the liquid as you can manage. The more liquid you can remove, the better the cakes with stay together.

2. Add the zucchini to the rest of the ingredients in a large bowl and stir together. The mixture should stay in a ball when you pinch it between your fingers. If it falls apart, try adding more flour, a tablespoon at a time.

3. Warm a heavy bottomed saucepan and add in a tablespoon of olive oil.

4. Form the patties into golf ball sized balls and then flatten them in your palm. Add the patties to the pan with enough space to flip them, but then don't adjust them. Cook for 5 minutes, until the first side is browned. Flip the patties carefully and cook for another 5 minutes on the second side. Serve warm.

Serves 4-6

Shake and Bake Tofu

The classic '80s dinner here when served with mashed potatoes and green peas! If you only have 30 minutes to pull something together, this is a great option. My daughter loves the crispy baked texture and I love that I don't have to get a bowl dirty.

Shake and Bake Tofu

Ingredients

¼ c. nutritional yeast

¼ c. corn meal

½ tsp. dried thyme

½ tsp. garlic powder

½ tsp. onion powder

½ tsp. salt (omit for <1)

Liquid from a can of beans

1 12 oz. package firm tofu

Spray olive oil

Instructions

1. Preheat the oven to 350 degrees F.

2. Fill a large ziploc bag with the nutritional yeast, corn meal, thyme, garlic powder, onion power, and salt.

3. Cut the tofu into sticks or chunks. One by one, dredge the tofu pieces into the chickpea liquid and then drop them into the bag of spices. I usually wait until I have 4- 5 pieces in the bag and then hold it closed and shake until the spice mix covers the tofu.

4. Carefully place the tofu on a baking sheet and continue dredging and shaking the tofu with the mixture.

5. Once you've gotten all the tofu covered, spray with the olive oil spray and bake for 20 minutes, flipping them over midway through. They should have a nice golden crust on them. If they look soggy, cook until you have a crust.

Serves 4

Black Bean Burgers

These are hearty and tasty black bean burgers that don't fall apart. You could even grill them; just flip them carefully to help them out a little.

Black Bean Burgers

Ingredients

1 c. cooked brown rice

1 c. walnuts, toasted

1 small onion, diced

1 garlic clove, minced

1 Tbsp. olive oil

1 tsp. cumin

½ tsp. salt

1 15oz. can black beans

⅓ c. breadcrumbs

3 Tbsp. tomato paste or organic ketchup

2 tsp. sugar

Instructions

1. In a large heavy bottomed saucepan, add the olive oil and onion and a pinch of salt and cook until the onions are translucent, about 5 minutes.

2. Add the walnuts, cumin, salt, and sugar to a blender and grind until it turns to flour. Add the beans and blend very briefly, just until combined. Don't over-process here.

3. Add the bean mixture, rice, breadcrumbs, and tomato paste in a large mixing bowl. Mix until it's really well combined. You should be able to grab a ball of it and it will stay together. If not, try adding more breadcrumbs a tablespoon at a time. If it seems too dry, try to add more tomato paste.

4. Form into small patties. Warm a skillet or grill pan and add just enough oil to the pan to cover it. Place the patties in the pan and cook on one side for 3-4 minutes. Carefully flip the patties and cook for another 3-4 minutes on the second side.

Serves 4

Red Wine Vinaigrette

Ingredients

¼ c. red wine vinegar

1 garlic clove, minced (or use ½ tsp. garlic powder)

1 Tbsp. Dijon mustard

1 Tbsp. maple syrup

½ tsp. dried oregano

¼ tsp. salt

2 Tbsp. extra virgin olive oil

Instructions

1. Combine the vinegar, garlic, mustard, maple syrup, and herbs in a small bowl.

2. Drizzle in the olive oil while whisking the dressing to emulsify the ingredients.

Balsamic Vinaigrette

Ingredients

¼ c. balsamic vinegar

1 clove garlic, minced (or use ½ tsp. garlic powder)

1 Tbsp. Dijon mustard

1 Tbsp. maple syrup

½ tsp. dried parsley

½ tsp. dried basil

½ tsp. dried oregano

¼ tsp. salt

2 Tbsp. extra virgin olive oil

Instructions

1. Combine the vinegar, garlic, mustard, maple syrup, and herbs in a small bowl.

2. Drizzle in the olive oil while continuing to whisk the dressing to emulsify the ingredients.

Serves 4-6

Lemon Dill Dressing

Ingredients

3 Tbsp. fresh lemon juice, about 1-2 lemons

1 Tbsp. Dijon mustard

1 garlic clove, minced (or use ½ tsp. garlic powder)

2 tsp. dried dill

pinch of salt and pepper (to taste)

2 Tbsp. extra virgin olive oil

Instructions

1. Whisk the lemon juice, mustard, garlic, dill, and salt together.

2. Then whisk the dressing while drizzling in the olive oil to combine the ingredients.

Raw Ranch Dressing

Ingredients

1½ c. raw cashews

2 Tbsp. fresh lemon juice

2 garlic cloves

1 stalk celery

1 tsp. sea salt (omit for under 1 year olds)

1½ tsp. onion powder

¾ c. water

½ tsp. dried dill

Instructions

1. Combine all the ingredients except the dill in a blender and blender until very smooth. I like to add the dill last so you can still see the flecks of green in the dressing. I feel like this is how old school ranch used to look, and if I blend it with everything else my Vitamix pulverizes it and you can barely see it. This is personal preference though and it's easier to do all in one shot.

2. If don't have a super powerful blender, I recommend soaking the cashews overnight in water (drain before adding to the blender), and starting your blender with the cashews and water. Then add the other ingredients.

Serves 4-6

Almond Dipping Sauce

This dip is amazing on grilled vegetables, but we use it for steamed, raw, sautéed , roasted ones too. I love it with broccoli.

Almond Dipping Sauce

Ingredients

½ c. almonds

¼ c. raisins

3 Tbsp. red wine vinegar

1½ Tbsp. Dijon mustard

1 shallot, chopped

1 garlic clove, chopped

½ c. olive oil

½ c. water

2 tsp. lemon juice

Instructions

1. Whisk everything together until blended. Taste for seasoning.

Serves 4-6

Roasted Garlic Hummus

Hummus is super basic, but this recipe has extra pizazz because of the roasted garlic. It's easy and can have added ingredients like roasted red peppers to jazz it up.

Roasted Garlic Hummus

Ingredients

2 garlic cloves

1 tsp. olive oil

1 15 oz. can of chickpeas

¼ c. tahini

2 Tbsp. fresh lemon juice

½ tsp. cumin

½ tsp. salt

¼ tsp. paprika

1 Tbsp. water or chickpea liquid, as needed

Instructions

1. Roast the garlic with the olive oil until lightly golden brown and fragrant. I like to use a little piece of aluminum foil and just put my garlic on it in the toaster oven. Don't let the garlic overcook; it should only take about 5 minutes to turn golden brown.

2. Combine all the ingredients in a strong blender and mix until smooth. Taste for salt and flavors.

Serves 4-6

Peanut Sauce

This peanut sauce is creamy, nutritious, and delicious. We typically add it on noodles, but you can see it's really great on any grain, bean, or vegetable dish you need to pack with flavor.

Peanut Sauce

Ingredients

1 12 oz. can coconut milk

¼ c. water

¼ c. maple syrup (you can omit if you don't want any sugar added)

¼ c. liquid aminos or coconut aminos

½ c. natural creamy peanut butter

1 tsp. grated ginger (or use ¼ tsp. dried ginger)

3 garlic cloves, minced or grated

2 Tbsp. lime juice

1 Tbsp. toasted sesame oil

Instructions

1. Combine all of the ingredients except the lime juice and sesame oil in a saucepan and bring to medium heat.

2. Cook for about 10 minutes, whisking frequently, until everything is combined and the sauce begins to thicken.

3. Remove from the heat and mix in the lime juice and sesame oil.

Serves 4-6

Alfredo Sauce

My daughter loves this creamy, savory sauce on pasta. Note that the more salt you add, the more it tends to taste like old school Alfredo, but with younger kids you'll want to avoid that much salt.

Alfredo Sauce

Ingredients

1 Tbsp. olive oil

1 onion, chopped

2 garlic cloves, chopped

1½ c. raw cashews

2 c. water

1 Tbsp. lemon juice

1 tsp. sea salt (omit for children under 1)

Instructions

1. Heat the olive oil and onion in a saucepan with a pinch of salt. Cook until the onions are translucent, about 5 minutes.

2. Add in the garlic and cook for 30 more seconds, and then remove from the heat.

3. Add the onions and garlic to the rest of the ingredients in a blender and whirl until creamy and smooth. If don't have a super powerful blender, I recommend soaking the cashews overnight in water (drain before adding to the blender), and starting your blender with the cashews and water. Then add the other ingredients.

Serves 4-6

Spaghetti Sauce

A simple, classic spaghetti sauce for pasta and pizza.

Spaghetti Sauce

Ingredients

1 Tbsp. olive oil

1 onion, chopped

1 carrot, chopped

1 celery stalk, chopped

4 garlic cloves, chopped

1 tsp. basil

1 tsp. oregano

1 tsp. thyme

1 tsp. parsley

1 tsp. salt (omit for under 1 years old)

1 28 oz. can of tomatoes

¼ c. almond or soy milk

Instructions

1. Heat the olive oil, onion, carrot, and celery with a pinch of salt over medium heat in a deep, heavy saucepan. Cook for about 10 minutes, until the vegetables are softened.

2. Add in the garlic, herbs, and salt, cook for about 30 seconds. Then add in the canned tomatoes. Bring to a boil and then reduce the heat to low and cook for at least 30 minutes.

3. When the sauce is done cooking, remove it from the heat and add it with the milk into a blender and blend until smooth.

Serves 4-6

Oozy Cheese Sauce

We use this oozy cheese sauce for mac-n-cheese, baked potatoes, grilled cheese sandwiches, homemade French fries, and as a dip for vegetables.

Oozy Cheese Sauce

Ingredients

3 medium Yukon gold or red potatoes

3" chunk of sweet potato

½ small red pepper

2 medium carrots

¼ onion, chopped

3 garlic cloves, peeled

1 tsp. olive oil

½ c. cashews

1 tsp. fresh lemon juice (or use half a lemon in the blender)

1 tsp. chickpea miso

1 tsp. prepared mustard

1 tsp. sea salt (omit for children under 1 year old)

Instructions

1. Fill a saucepot with water and bring to a boil with the potatoes, sweet potato, pepper, carrots, and onion. When the vegetables are tender, about 20-25 minutes later, remove them from the water. You might want to save some water to thin out the sauce later if it gets too thick, so I don't drain it quite yet.

2. While the vegetables are cooking, roast the garlic with the olive oil for a few minutes until it's fragrant and light brown. I put it in my toaster oven on 400 degrees for about 10 minutes, but watch it in yours to make sure it doesn't burn.

3. Put the cooked vegetables, roasted garlic, cashews, lemon (or lemon juice), miso, mustard, and salt into a high-speed blender and blend until the mixture is smooth and creamy. If it gets thicker than you like, add in some of the reserved cooking water.

4. Note: If you don't have a powerful blender, I would go slowly with this, starting with the potatoes, then adding the other cooked vegetables and garlic, adding the cashews next, and then adding the remaining ingredients.

Serves 4-6

Ladybug Apples

This cute and fun recipe is perfect for toddlers who love bugs and are difficult to get to sit still and be interested in eating when the world is so much more fun.

Ladybug Apples

Ingredients

1 apple

1 Tbsp. nut butter (peanut butter sticks the best)

1-2 Tbsp. raisins

Instructions

1. Cut the apple in half and remove the core. Put dollops of nut butter on the apple and stick raisins on top.

Serves 1-2

Chia Seed Pudding

Chia seeds are packed with nutrients, and they make a fun popping feeling in a child's mouth, so they are great for working on eating lots of textures. You can add granola for a great breakfast option too.

128

Chia Seed Pudding

Ingredients

½ c. chia seeds

2 c. nondairy milk

1 tsp. vanilla

2 Tbsp. maple syrup (optional, I didn't use this until she was 2 years old)

¼ tsp. cinnamon (optional)

Instructions

1. Mix all the ingredients together in a Tupperware container and shake a couple times to encourage the seeds to absorb the moisture.

2. Refrigerate for several hours until the chia seeds have absorbed most of the liquid and everything is cold and thickened. I just make it at night and serve it for breakfast.

Serves 2-3

Ambrosia Salad

This is another '80s throwback dish, but without the sour cream and marshmallows. I used to love that snack, but this one is so much better. Real oranges are a step up from the canned Mandarins.

Ambrosia Salad

Ingredients

½ c. unsweetened organic coconut milk yogurt

1 Clementine or small organic orange, segmented

¼ c. chopped pineapple

1 Tbsp. organic coconut flakes

Instructions

1. Stir the yogurt, orange, and pineapple together and then top with coconut flakes.

Serves 1

Fruit and Yogurt Parfait

You can make parfaits with just about any fruit, but I love them with soft, sweet fruits like berries, bananas, peaches, or pineapple.

Fruit and Yogurt Parfait

Ingredients

1 c. unsweetened organic nondairy yogurt

½ c. assorted organic berries

½ c. organic oats (or use some homemade granola, see my recipe)

1 Tbsp. chia seeds (hemp or flax work nicely too)

Instructions

1. Put a layer of yogurt on the bottoms of two parfait dishes, or bowls.

2. Put in about half of the fruit on the next layer, then half the oats on top.

3. Add a second layer of yogurt and a second layer of both fruit and oats.

4. Top everything off with the sprinkle of chia seeds.

Serves 2

Homemade Granola

Once you have a basic recipe for granola like this one down, you can really change it up however you like. Oats, nuts, fruit, and oil are all you need.

Homemade Granola

Ingredients

4 c. rolled oats

1 c. shredded coconut

1 c. sliced almonds

¼ c. coconut oil, melted

1 Tbsp. cinnamon

1½ tsp. vanilla extract

pinch of salt (or omit for under 1 years old)

½ c. dried fruit

Instructions

1. Preheat the oven to 350 degrees F.

2. Combine all of the ingredients except the fruit in a large mixing bowl, stirring to thoroughly incorporate everything. Spread it into a thin layer on a baking sheet.

3. Put in the oven to bake for 30 minutes, stirring a few times. The oats should be golden brown and crispy when the granola is cooked. Fold in the dried fruit and allow to cool before eating.

4. You can store granola in an airtight container for a week.

Serves 8

Lemon Mint Fruit Salad

You can make fruit salad with any fruit you have on hand. I personally like to use sturdy fruit like berries, grapes, citrus, and melons, and I stay away from soft things like bananas and mangoes.

Lemon Mint Fruit Salad

Ingredients

12 oz. Strawberries

8 oz. blueberries

8 oz. blackberries

12 oz. grapes (or a bowl full of washed and sliced fruit you have left over)

1 lemon, juiced

1 tsp. vanilla extract

handful of mint, chopped

Instructions

1. Wash the fruit and cut it into bite-sized pieces.

2. Combine the lemon juice, vanilla, and mint and stir well.

3. Pour the dressing over the salad and serve!

4. You can garnish with pieces of mint, and have your toddler smell the mint pieces and taste them and see what it's like to chew mint leaves

Serves 8

Recipe Index

Recipe Index

Made in United States
Orlando, FL
19 August 2023

36246771R10082